Super Simple
Cultural Art

# Super Simple
# AFRiCAN ARt

## Fun and Easy Art from Around the World

## Alex Kuskowski

Consulting Editor, Diane Craig, M.A./Reading Specialist

A Division of ABDO

ABDO
Publishing Company

# visit us at www.abdopublishing.com

Published by ABDO Publishing Company, a division of ABDO, P.O. Box 398166, Minneapolis, Minnesota 55439. Copyright © 2012 by Abdo Consulting Group, Inc. International copyrights reserved in all countries. No part of this book may be reproduced in any form without written permission from the publisher. Super SandCastle™ is a trademark and logo of ABDO Publishing Company.

Printed in the United States of America, North Mankato, Minnesota
102011
012012

♻ PRINTED ON RECYCLED PAPER

Editor: Liz Salzmann
Content Developer: Nancy Tuminelly
Interior Design and Production: Oona Gaarder-Juntti, Mighty Media, Inc.
Cover Design: Kelsey Gullickson, Mighty Media, Inc.
Photo Credits: Comstock Images, Hemera Technologies, Jupiterimages, Shutterstock, Thinkstock

The following manufacturers/names appearing in this book are trademarks:
Color™ Duck Tape®, Crayola® Model Magic®, Elmer's® Glue-All™, Fiskars®, Glitter Glue™, Paper Mate®, Quaker®, Sharpie®, Tulip® Matte® Soft Fabric Paint™

**Library of Congress Cataloging-in-Publication Data**
Kuskowski, Alex.
  Super simple African art : fun and easy art from around the world / Alex Kuskowski.
     p. cm. -- (Super simple cultural art)
  ISBN 978-1-61783-210-9
  1.  Handicraft--Juvenile literature. 2.  Africa--Civilization--Miscellanea--Juvenile literature.  I. Title.
  TT160.K873 2012
  745.5--dc23
                    2011024600

Super SandCastle™ books are created by a team of professional educators, reading specialists, and content developers around five essential components—phonemic awareness, phonics, vocabulary, text comprehension, and fluency—to assist young readers as they develop reading skills and strategies and increase their general knowledge. All books are written, reviewed, and leveled for guided reading, early reading intervention, and Accelerated Reader® programs for use in shared, guided, and independent reading and writing activities to support a balanced approach to literacy instruction.

## TO ADULT HELPERS

Children can have a lot of fun learning about different cultures through arts and crafts. Be sure to supervise them as they work on the projects in this book. Let the kids do as much as possible on their own. But be ready to step in and help if necessary. Also, kids may be using glue, paint, markers, and clay. Make sure they protect their clothes and work surfaces.

## Symbol

**ADULT HELPER**
Ask for help. You will need help from an adult.

# Table of Contents

## Mask

Many tribes in Africa make masks. They can have human or animal faces. The masks are worn during dances and celebrations.

# Art Around the World

People from around the world do things differently. That's because of their **culture**. Everyone belongs to a culture, even you! Learning about different cultures can be a lot of fun.

Each culture has its own way of doing things. Often the things people make show a certain style. Try some of the art projects in this book. See what you can learn about African culture! You can even share what you learn with others.

## African Drum

Drums are a big part of most African music. The different beats and sounds can have special meanings.

# Before You Start

Remember to treat other people and **cultures** with respect. Respect their art, **jewelry**, and clothes too. These things can have special meaning to people.

There are a few rules for doing art projects.

- **Permission**
  Make sure to ask permission to do a project. You might want to use things you find around the house. Ask first!

- **Safety**
  Get help from an adult when using something hot or sharp. Never use an oven by yourself.

### Mkeka

Mkeka (em-kay-kah) means "mat" in the Swahili language. An mkeka is made of straw or cloth. It is one of the **symbols** of **Kwanzaa**. Other Kwanzaa symbols are arranged on top of the mkeka.

# Art in African Culture

People in Africa create many beautiful things. Some are for everyday use. Others are for special occasions. The **designs** in African art often have special meanings.

## Masai Collar Necklace

**Masai** women in **Kenya** wear a lot of beaded **jewelry**. This is not just because it's pretty. Each color of bead has a special meaning. Owning beads also shows that a person is wealthy or important.

## Hamsa Hand

Arabic is the main language of North Africa. Hamsa means "five" in Arabic. A hamsa hand often has an eye on it. Hamsa hands are worn for good luck.

## Warrior Shield

Many African **warriors** and hunters carried **shields**. The shields often had special **symbols** on them.

# Materials

Here are some of the materials you'll need to get started.

tape

pencil

plastic fork

construction paper

oatmeal container

paint pens

markers

glitter glue

ruler

cardboard

paintbrushes

glue

colored duct tape

8

key rings

paper plates

black string

beads

craft foam

bowls, different sizes

black fabric paint

scissors

hole punch

toothpicks

T-shirt

elastic cord

air-drying clay

ribbon

acrylic paint

9

# COLORFUL PAPER MKEKA

Make an mkeka for a Kwanzaa celebration!

Fold a piece of construction paper in half crosswise.

 Draw a line along the edge opposite the fold. The line should be 1 inch (3 cm) from the edge.

 Make small marks 1 inch (3 cm) apart along the line. Also make small marks 1 inch (3 cm) apart along the fold. Draw straight lines between the sets of marks.

 Cut along the lines from the fold up to the line. Unfold the paper. This is the base of the mkeka.

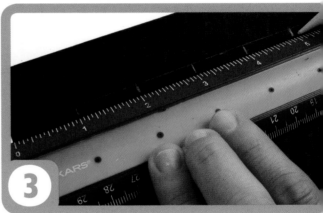

 Choose a few colors of paper. Draw lines the short way across each sheet. The lines should be 1 inch (3 cm) apart.

 Cut on the lines. This makes strips of paper. Cut some of the strips in half lengthwise.

**7** Lay the base sheet on the table. Make sure the pencil marks are face down. Push a strip through the first cut in the base.

**Weave** the strip in and out of the cuts.

 Push the strip all the way to one side.

 Weave more strips across the base sheet. Use different colors and sizes. Push each new strip close to the last one.

 Add strips until the base is full. Then glue the ends of the strips to the base.

 Cut off the ends of any strips that stick out.

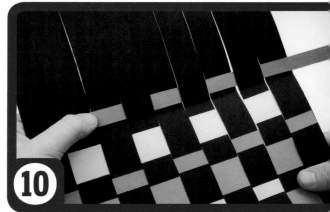

# COOL KUFi CAP

**WHAT YOU NEED**
- construction paper
- ruler
- scissors
- glue

Kufi caps are part of the national costume in many West African countries.

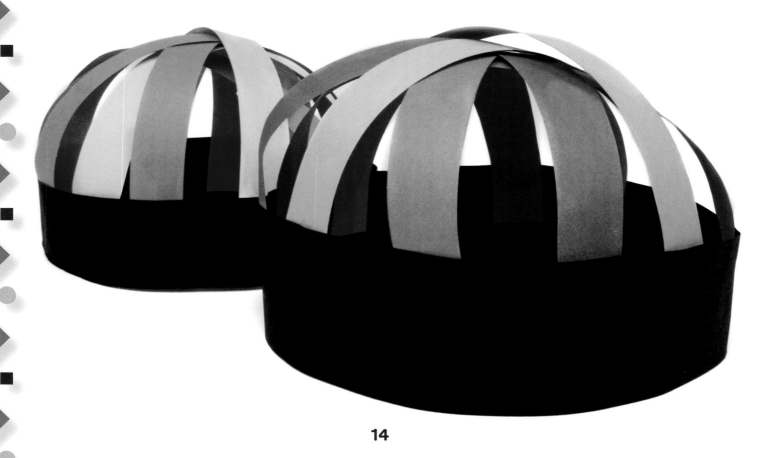

**1** Cut six strips of colored paper. They should be 12 inches (30 cm) by 1 inch (3 cm).

 **2** Lay the strips on top of each other. They should all cross in the middle

 **3** Cut a large strip of black paper. Glue the ends together to make a circle. Make sure it fits around your head.

 **4** Set the black band on the colored strips. Glue the ends of the strips to the band. Glue them on the inside.

**5** Turn the cap over. Let the glue dry. Wear your kufi cap with pride!

15

# AFRICAN DRUM

Make an African drum. You'll bring a new beat to your house!

**WHAT YOU NEED**
• construction paper
• scissors
• oatmeal container
• tape
• colored duct tape
• markers

**1** Cut a piece of paper in half lengthwise. Wrap one half around the oatmeal container. Tape the ends.

**2** Cover the rest of the container with duct tape. Wrap the tape smoothly. Make sure the label is completely covered.

**3** Does the lid have a label? Cover it with tape or a circle of paper.

**4** Use markers to decorate the drum. Draw colorful **designs** and patterns.

**5** Hold the drum under your arm. Start drumming!

# ADINKRA T-SHIRT

Decorate a shirt using adinkra symbols from Ghana.

**1** Put a piece of cardboard inside the T-shirt. This will keep the shirt flat and smooth.

**2** Pour some fabric paint onto a paper plate. Dip a plastic fork into the paint. Drag the fork across the shirt. Make four rows. The paint might run out. Just dip the fork in the paint again. Continue the line from where the paint ran out.

**3** Draw four more lines in the other direction. This makes a grid pattern.

**4** Choose **symbols** to put on your shirt. Look up adinkra symbols online for ideas. Or make up your own symbols.

**5** Draw the symbols on craft foam. Cut them out.

19

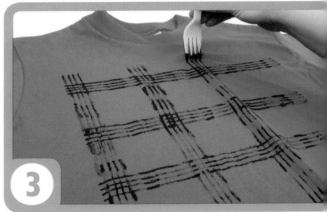

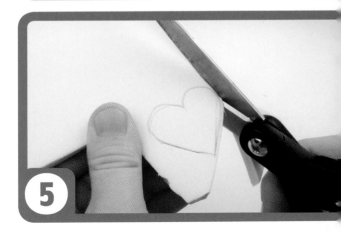

 **6** Cut pieces of cardboard. They should be a little larger than the foam **symbols**. Glue each symbol to a piece of cardboard.

 **7** Dip a symbol into the fabric paint. Hold it by the cardboard.

 **8** Press the symbol onto the shirt. Stamp a symbol inside each square. Create a pattern with the different symbols.

**9** Let the paint dry completely. Then you can wear your adinkra T-shirt!

20

# TRiBaL Mask

Make a mask that celebrates something or someone important.

**WHAT YOU NEED**
- large sheet of cardboard
- pencil
- scissors
- large piece of paper
- acrylic paint
- paintbrush
- markers
- glitter glue
- hole punch
- elastic cord

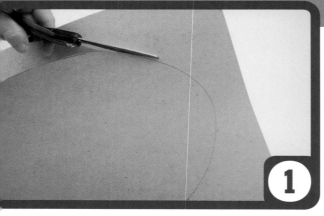

 Draw an oval on the cardboard. It should be as big as your head. Cut out the oval.

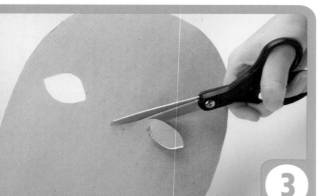

 Trace the cardboard oval on paper. Cut it out. Hold the paper oval in front of your face. Have an adult carefully draw around your eyes. Cut out the eyes.

 Lay the paper oval on the cardboard oval. Trace the eye holes onto the cardboard. Cut the eye holes out of the cardboard.

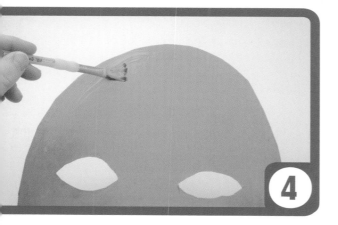

Paint the mask a solid color. Let the paint dry.

Use a black marker to draw a **design** on the mask. Practice drawing your ideas on paper first.

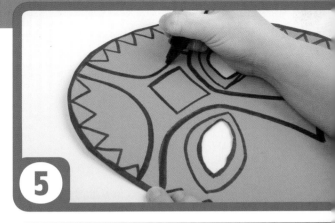

 Use paint and markers to color in the design. Decorate the mask with glitter glue. Let the paint and glue dry.

 Punch a hole on each side of the mask.

Cut a piece of elastic cord. Tie one end of the cord to each of the holes. Make sure it is tight enough to hold the mask on.

 Make up a dance to do while wearing your mask!

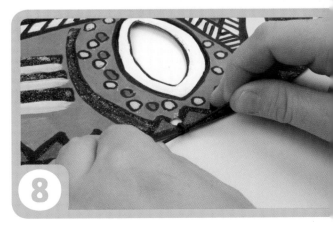

# WARRIOR'S SHIELD

Make a shield to protect yourself from dangerous beasts!

**WHAT YOU NEED**
- large sheet of cardboard
- markers
- construction paper
- ruler
- scissors
- glue
- acrylic paint
- paintbrush
- glitter glue

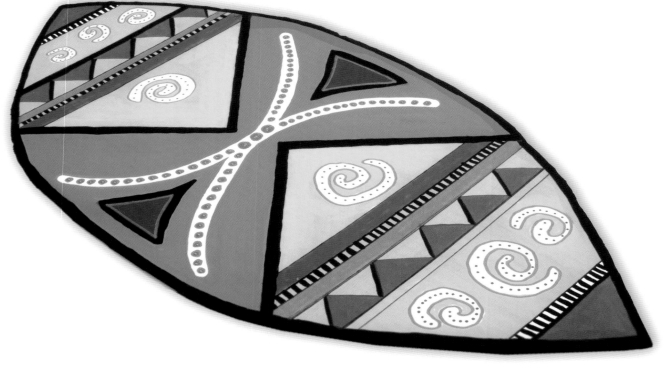

1. Draw the shape of the **shield** on the cardboard. Make it as big as you can! Try a long oval with points at the ends. That is the shape of a **Zulu** shield.

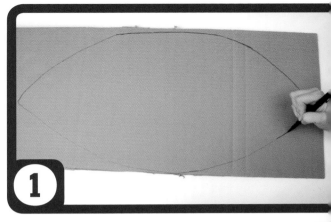

2. Cut out the shield. Lay your arm across the back of the shield. Draw lines along both sides of your arm.

3. Cut two strips of paper. They should be 5 inches (13 cm) by 2 inches (5 cm).

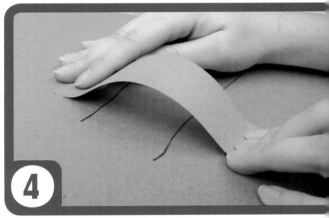

4. Glue the strips over the lines. Make sure your arm fits under them. Put the strips about 2 inches (5 cm) apart. Wait for the glue to dry.

5. Decorate the shield. Use paint, markers, and glitter glue. Make up your own **designs**!

# Masai collar Necklace

Make your own Masai jewelry.

**WHAT YOU NEED**
- cardboard
- 2 bowls, different sizes
- pencil
- scissors
- ruler
- markers
- acrylic paint
- paintbrush
- paint pens
- glitter glue
- ribbon
- tape

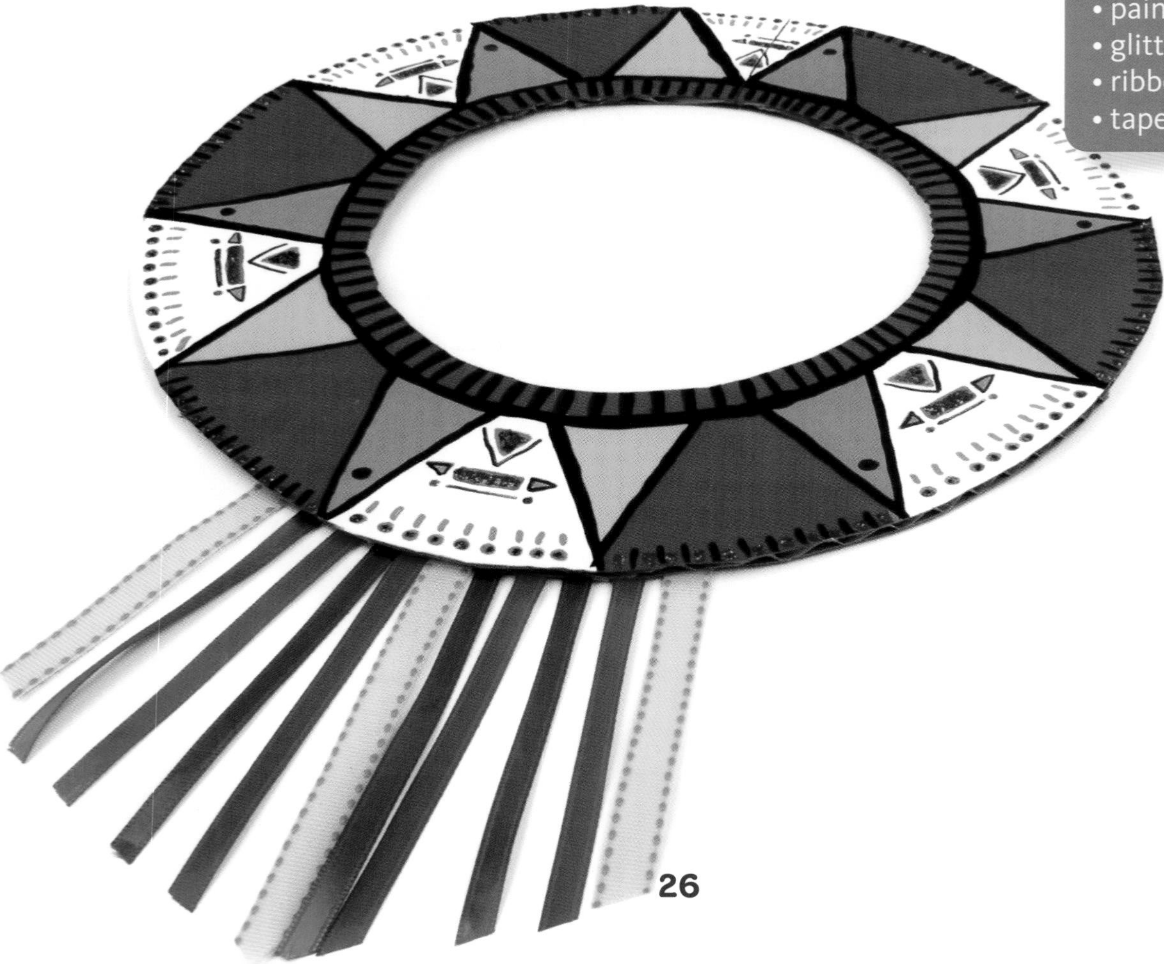

26

**1** Put the large bowl upside down on the cardboard. Trace around it.

 **2** Put the small bowl upside down inside the circle. Trace around it.

**3** Cut out the big circle. Then cut from the outside edge to the center circle. Cut out the center circle.

**4** Decorate the necklace. Use a ruler to draw triangles. Color them with markers, paint, or paint pens. Add glitter glue **designs**. Let it dry.

**5** Cut some ribbons about 5 inches (13 cm) long. Tape them to the back of the necklace. Cut the ends so they make a V.

**6** Twist open the cut in the circle. Slip it around your neck!

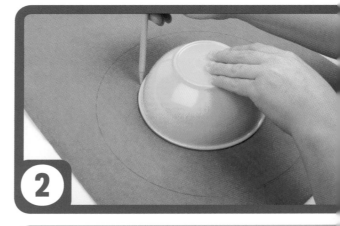

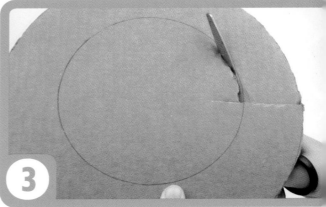

# HAMSA KEY CHAIN

Make a hamsa key chain. You'll carry good luck around!

Shape the clay into a hand. Make it about 1 inch (3 cm).

 Stick the toothpick through the hand. Make a hole for a string to fit through. Let the clay dry.

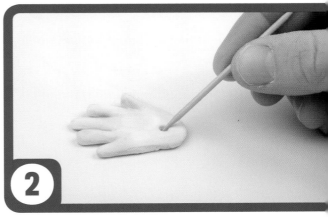 Paint the hand. Paint one side and let it dry. Then paint the other side. Let it dry.

 Hamsa hands are often decorated. One common decoration is an eye. Use a marker to decorate the hand.

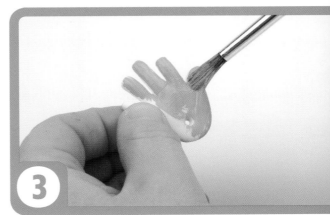

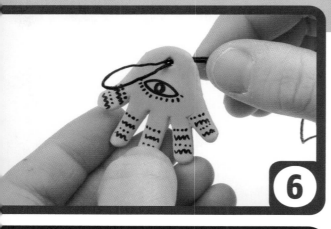

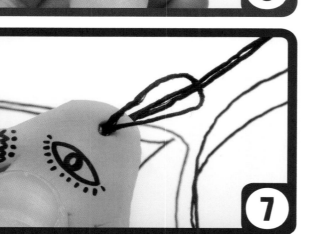

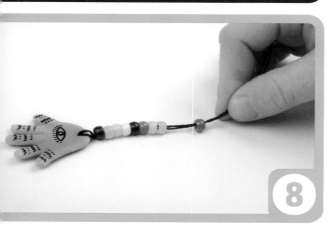

**5** Cut a piece of string about 36 inches (91 cm) long.

**6** Fold the string in half. Put the folded end through the hole in the hand.

**7** Put the ends of the string through the fold. Pull so the string is tight against the hand.

**8** Put beads on the strings. Put both strings through each bead. Add about 2½ inches (6 cm) of beads. Tie a knot after the last bead.

Put 8 to 10 more beads on the strings. Put both strings through each bead.

 Put the ends of the string through the key ring.

 Hold the first bead after the knot. Put the ends of the string back through this bead.

**12** Pull the strings tight. The beads should wrap around the ring. Tie a double knot. Cut off the extra string.

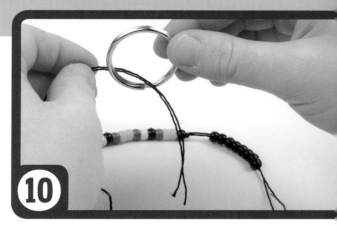

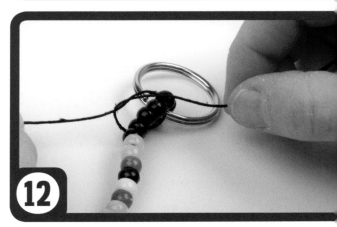

# Conclusion

Did you learn about African **culture**? Did you have fun making these art projects? Learning about other cultures is very interesting. You can learn about how people around the world live. Try looking up more **information** about Africans!

# Glossary

**culture** – the ideas, traditions, art, and behaviors of a group of people.

**design** – a decorative pattern or arrangement.

**information** – the facts known about an event or subject.

**jewelry** – pretty things, such as rings, necklaces, and bracelets, that you wear for decoration.

**Kenya** – a country in East Africa.

**Kwanzaa** – an American holiday that honors African-American culture and heritage.

**Masai** – a large ethnic group in Kenya and Tanzania.

**shield** – something that keeps harmful things from reaching someone.

**symbol** – an object or picture that stands for or represents something.

**warrior** – a person who fights in a war or battle.

**weave** – to make something by passing strips of material over and under each other.

**Zulu** – a large ethnic group in South Africa.